Course Editor
Rabbi Michoel Shapiro

Curriculum Development
Rabbi Mordechai Dinerman
Rabbi Naftali Silberberg

Mythbusters
is largely based on the content of the JLI course
Fascinating Facts
authored by
Rivkah Slonim and **Rabbi Avrohom Sternberg**
edited and produced by
Rabbi Naftali Silberberg and **Chana Silberstein, PhD**

Printed in the United States of America
© Published and Copyrighted 2016 by
The Rohr Jewish Learning Institute
822 Eastern Parkway, Brooklyn, NY 11213

All rights reserved.
No part of the contents of this book
may be reproduced or transmitted in any form
or by any means
without the written permission of the publisher.

(888) YOUR-JLI/718-221-6900
www.myJLI.com

ב"ה

JLI TEENS *discovery* program

Book Three

MYTHBUSTERS

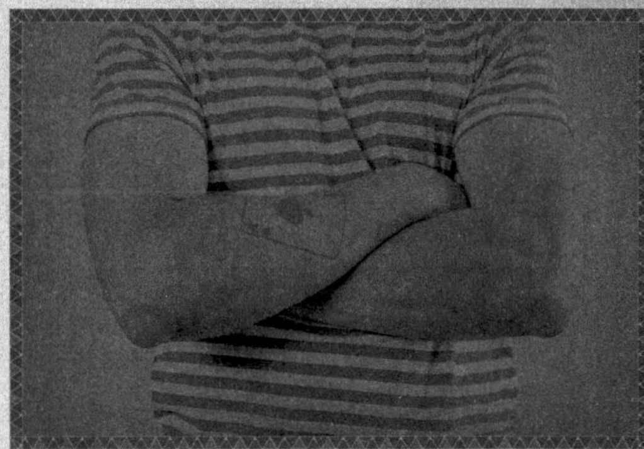

MYTHBUSTERS

The Rohr Jewish Learning Institute acknowledges the generous support of the following individuals and foundations

PRINCIPAL BENEFACTOR

GEORGE ROHR
New York, NY

ADVISORY BOARD OF GOVERNORS

YAAKOV AND KAREN COHEN
Potomac, MD

YITZCHOK AND JULIE GNIWISCH
Montreal, QC

BARBARA HINES
Aspen, CO

DANIEL B. MARKSON
S. Antonio, TX

DANIEL AND ROSIE MATTIO
Seattle, WA

DAVID MINTZ
Tenafly, NJ

DR. STEPHEN F. SERBIN
Columbia, SC

LEONARD A. WIEN, JR.
Miami Beach, FL

PILLARS OF JEWISH LITERACY

KEVIN BERMEISTER
Sydney, Australia

PABLO AND SARA BRIMAN
Mexico City, Mexico

YOSEF GOROWITZ
Redondo Beach, CA

DR. VERA KOCH GROSZMANN
S. Paulo, Brazil

HERSCHEL LAZAROFF
Baltimore, MD

JENNY LJUNGBERG
New York, NY

DAVID MAGERMAN
Gladwyne, PA

DR. MICHAEL MALING
Deerfield, IL

YITZCHAK MIRILASHVILI
Herzliya, Israel

LARRY SIFEN
Virginia Beach, VA

YAIR SHAMIR
Savyon, Israel

PARTNERING FOUNDATIONS

WILLIAM DAVIDSON FOUNDATION

MEROMIM FOUNDATION

KOHELET FOUNDATION

CRAIN-MALING FOUNDATION

WORLD ZIONIST ORGANIZATION

AVI CHAI FOUNDATION

OLAMI WORLDWIDE - WOLFSON FOUNDATION

RUDERMAN FAMILY FOUNDATION

THE ESTATE OF ELLIOT JAMES BELKIN

SPONSORS

MARK AND REBECCA BOLINSKY
Long Beach, NY

DANIEL AND ETA COTLAR
Houston, TX

SHMUEL AND SHARONE GOODMAN
Chicago, IL

FRANK AND FRUMETH POLASKY
Saginaw, MI

DR. ZE'EV RAV-NOY
Los Angeles, CA

ALAN ZEKELMAN
Bloomfield Hills, MI

The **Rohr Jewish Learning Institute**
gratefully acknowledges the pioneering support of

George and Pamela Rohr

SINCE ITS INCEPTION,
the **Rohr JLI** has been a beneficiary of the vision,
generosity, care, and concern of the **Rohr family**

In the merit of the tens of thousands of hours of Torah study
by **JLI** students worldwide, may they be blessed with health,
Yiddishe nachas from all their loved ones, and extraordinary success
in all their endeavors

Dedicated to

Frank and Frumeth Polasky

Dear friends of JLI

With deep appreciation for their partnership with JLI
and leadership in bringing Torah study
to all corners of the world.

May they be blessed with much health, happiness, success,
and abundance in all their endeavors as they go from strength to strength
in their service of G-d, the Jewish people, and humanity.

On behalf of the leadership and administration
of the Rohr Jewish Learning Institute (JLI)

TABLE OF CONTENTS

Lesson One

MYTH BUSTERS OF BIBLICAL PROPORTIONS

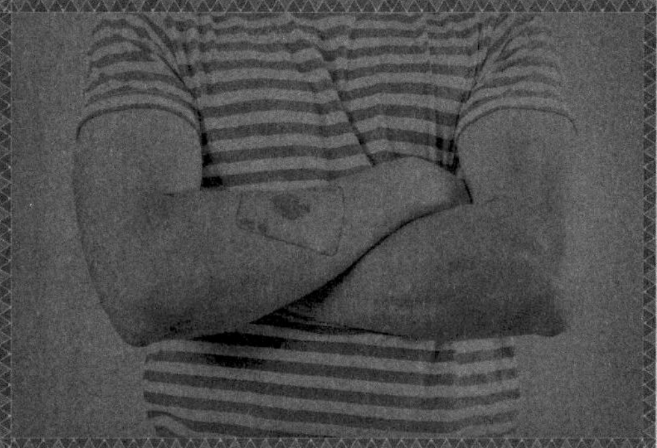

MythBUSTERS

2

THE FORBIDDEN FRUIT

A TALE OF TWO TREES

EXERCISE 1

When Adam and Chavah sinned by eating from the Tree of Knowledge, what fruit did they eat?

A. Apple

B. Fig

C. Grape

D. Orange

TEXT 1

וַיַּצְמַח ה' אֱלֹקִים מִן הָאֲדָמָה כָּל עֵץ נֶחְמָד לְמַרְאֶה וְטוֹב
לְמַאֲכָל, וְעֵץ הַחַיִּים בְּתוֹךְ הַגָּן וְעֵץ הַדַּעַת טוֹב וָרָע . . .

וַיְצַו ה' אֱלֹקִים עַל הָאָדָם לֵאמֹר, "מִכֹּל עֵץ הַגָּן אָכֹל תֹּאכֵל. וּמֵעֵץ
הַדַּעַת טוֹב וָרָע לֹא תֹאכַל מִמֶּנּוּ, כִּי בְּיוֹם אֲכָלְךָ מִמֶּנּוּ מוֹת תָּמוּת".

And the Lord God caused to sprout from the ground every tree that was pleasant to see and good to eat, and, in the midst of the garden, the Tree of Life and the Tree of Knowledge of Good and Evil. . . .

And the Lord God commanded man, saying, "Of every tree of the garden you may freely eat. But of the Tree of Knowledge of Good and Evil you shall not eat, for you shall surely die on the day that you eat thereof."

Bereishit 2:9, 16–17

KEY POINT

QUESTION FOR DISCUSSION

Can you think of biblical clues to support any of these positions?

TEXT 2

The tree from which Adam ate:

Rabbi Meir says it was a grapevine. . . .

Rabbi Nechemiah says it was a fig tree. . . .

Rabbi Yehudah says it was a wheat stalk.

Talmud, Berachot 40a

FIGURE 1.1

Myth	The fruit of the Tree of Knowledge was an apple.
Fact	

WHAT'S THE DIFFERENCE TO ME?

TEXT 3

Rabbi Azariah and Rabbi Yehudah ben Simon said in the name of Rabbi Yehoshu'a ben Levi: ". . . God never revealed the identity of the tree to any man, and He never will. . . . [For,] if God is anxious to safeguard the dignity of the average human being, how much more so the dignity of Adam and Chavah!"

Midrash, Bereishit Rabah 15:7

KEY POINT

TEXT 4

Woe to the person who says that the Torah's objective is merely to relate stories and mundane tales. . . . If the objective of the Torah were to relate historical matters, the rulers of the world have historical chronicles that are superior; let us utilize them and produce from them a [better] Torah!

Zohar 3:152a

KEY POINT

THE THORNY PROBLEM

TEXT 5A

וַיֵּרָא מַלְאַךְ ה' אֵלָיו בְּלַבַּת אֵשׁ מִתּוֹךְ הַסְּנֶה. וַיַּרְא,
וְהִנֵּה הַסְּנֶה בֹּעֵר בָּאֵשׁ וְהַסְּנֶה אֵינֶנּוּ אֻכָּל.

An angel of God appeared to [Moshe] in the heart of a fire in the midst of the thornbush. Moshe looked, and behold, the thornbush was ablaze, but the thornbush was not consumed.

Shemot 3:2

KEY POINT

TEXT 5B

"I am with [Israel] in their distress" (Tehilim 91:15). God said to Moshe, "Do you not realize that I am distressed just as the Jewish people are distressed [in their bondage]? Take note whence I am communicating with you–from within the thornbush," as if to say, "I am a partner in their distress."

Midrash, Shemot Rabah 2:5

TABLET TOPS

THE TEN COMMANDMENTS: WHAT DID THEY LOOK LIKE?

EXERCISE 2

Have you ever seen an illustration of the tablets containing the Ten Commandments? Try to draw what they looked like.

QUESTION FOR DISCUSSION

Does this text support or negate the possibility of the tablets having rounded tops?

TEXT 6

The ark that Moshe constructed was two-and-a-half cubits in length, one-and-a-half cubits in width, and one-and-a-half cubits in height. . . . Each of the tablets was six [handbreadths] long, six [handbreadths] wide, and three [handbreadths] deep, lying along the length of the ark.

Talmud, Bava Batra 14a

QUESTION FOR DISCUSSION

What additional information is provided in this text that conclusively indicates that the tablets were square-shaped?

TEXT 7

The tablets were square: six handbreadths long and six handbreadths wide. . . . If you study the dimensions of the tablets—the height, width, and depth—you will find that each tablet contained 108 cubic handbreadths.

Rabbi Bachaye ben Asher, Shemot 31:18

FIGURE 1.2

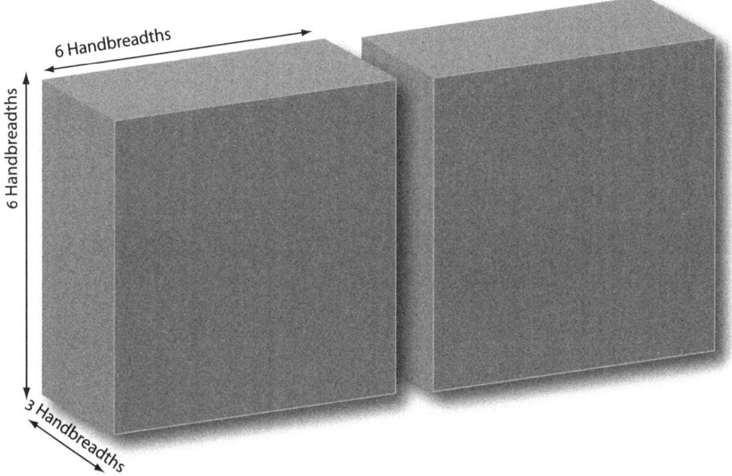

$6 \times 6 \times 3 = 108$

TEXT 8

The current standard perception of the Tablets derives from Christian art. . . . In Italy, from ancient times through Romanesque and Gothic periods and up until the 16th century, the *Luchot* were portrayed as two rectangular tablets. In France, from at least the 12th century, it was the familiar rounded form that at a certain point supplanted all

KEY POINT

the other forms; so much so that from the 16th century on it is almost impossible to find Tablets represented in any other fashion.

Scholars have traced the origin of this form with relative ease. There are several features that almost always go together that betray its source. When portrayed as rectangular, the Tablets are always separate. When they have a rounded top, they are usually adjacent and even attached. Furthermore, when rounded they usually have a frame. All of these indicate a familiar form—the diptych. The diptych was an ancient writing tablet having two hinged leaves that was used in various forms through the Middle Ages. Representing the *Luchot* as a diptych lies in its use as a writing tablet, and probably originated in England, where the earliest extant example of rounded *Luchot* can be found in an 11th-century manuscript.

Rabbi Ari Z. Zivotofsky, "What's the Truth About . . . the Luchot?" *Jewish Action*, Summer 1998

FIGURE 1.3

Myth	The *luchot* were rectangularly shaped with rounded tops.
Fact	

BYLAWS OR MY LAWS?

FIGURE 1.4

1. I am Hashem, your God.

2. You shall have no other god besides me.

3. You shall not take the name of Hashem in vain.

4. Remember the Shabbat, to keep it holy.

5. Honor your father and your mother.

6. You shall not murder.

7. You shall not commit adultery.

8. You shall not steal.

9. You shall not bear false witness against your neighbor.

10. You shall not covet your neighbor's possessions.

THE STRANGEST MYTH

JEWISH HORNS

KEY POINT

CASE STUDY

In 2004, British comedian Sacha Baron Cohen published a video segment of himself posed as a fictional character named Borat Sagdiyev. This character, who claimed to be a foreigner hailing from the country of Kazakhstan, was visiting a country music club in Tucson, Arizona. Cohen, who is Jewish, sang a virulently anti-Semitic song to an unsuspecting American audience, claiming that in his country there is a "problem" called the "Jew" who takes everyone's money. The chorus urged his listeners to "throw the Jew down the well so my country can be free!" As he sang, Cohen managed to influence much of the club's patronage to cheer and sing along.

TEXT 9A

וַיְהִי בְּרֶדֶת מֹשֶׁה מֵהַר סִינַי וּשְׁנֵי לֻחֹת הָעֵדֻת בְּיַד מֹשֶׁה בְּרִדְתּוֹ מִן הָהָר, וּמֹשֶׁה לֹא יָדַע כִּי קָרַן עוֹר פָּנָיו בְּדַבְּרוֹ אִתּוֹ. וַיַּרְא אַהֲרֹן וְכָל בְּנֵי יִשְׂרָאֵל אֶת מֹשֶׁה וְהִנֵּה קָרַן עוֹר פָּנָיו, וַיִּירְאוּ מִגֶּשֶׁת אֵלָיו.

When Moshe descended from Mount Sinai, the two tablets of the testimony were in his hand as he descended from the mountain. And Moshe did not know that the skin of his face had become radiant (*karan*) when [God] spoke with him. Aharon and all of the Children of Israel saw Moshe and, behold, the skin of his face was radiant, and they were afraid to approach him.

Shemot 34:29–30

KEY POINT

TEXT 9B

When Moses came down from Mount Sinai, he held the two tablets of the testimony, and he knew not that his face was horned from the conversation of the Lord.

Vulgate, Exodus 34:29

KEY POINT

FIGURE 1.5

Myth	The Jewish leader, Moshe, is portrayed in the Torah as having horns.
Fact	

RADIANT YOU

QUESTION FOR DISCUSSION

Can you justify this Talmudic statement?

TEXT 10

The heights achieved by those who repent cannot be attained even by those who are perfectly righteous.

Talmud, Berachot 34b

Lesson Two

KOSHER FACT AND FICTION

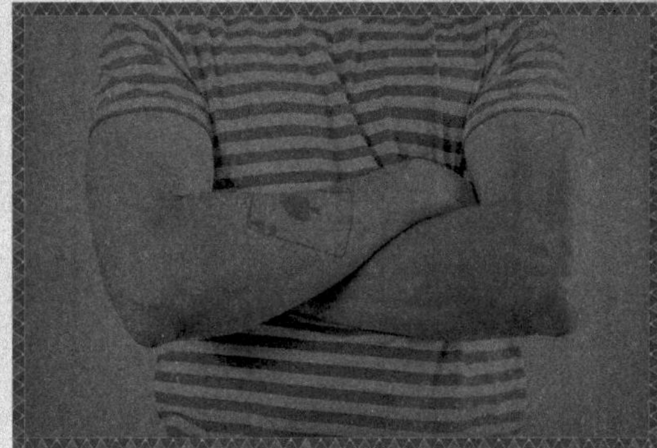

MYTHBUSTERS

KOSHER: WHAT IS IT?

EXERCISE 1

What does "kosher food" mean?

A. Jewish ethnic cuisine

B. Food that was blessed by a rabbi

C. Food produced under rabbinical supervision

D. Food that is suitable to eat

KOSHER = HEALTHY?

THE MYTH

EXERCISE 2

Complete the following sentence:

Kosher food is . . .

A. . . . cleaner.

B. . . . more nutritious.

C. . . . more delicious.

D. . . . a high standard of food quality.

TEXT 1

Christians, Muslims, Jews and Atheists alike are helping fuel the robust market for kosher foods, according to a new report by market research firm Mintel. In a consumer survey of adults who purchase kosher food, Mintel found that the number one reason people buy kosher is for food quality (62%).

KEY POINT

The second most common reason people say they purchase kosher food is "general healthfulness" (51%) and the third is food safety (34%). This contrasts sharply to the just 14% of respondents who say they purchase kosher food because they follow kosher religious rules.

Another 10% buy kosher because they follow some other religious rules with eating restrictions similar to kosher.

Mintel Press Release, February 2009

EAT JEWISH

TEXT 2

וַיְדַבֵּר ה׳ אֶל מֹשֶׁה וְאֶל אַהֲרֹן לֵאמֹר אֲלֵהֶם:

דַּבְּרוּ אֶל בְּנֵי יִשְׂרָאֵל לֵאמֹר זֹאת הַחַיָּה אֲשֶׁר תֹּאכְלוּ מִכָּל
הַבְּהֵמָה אֲשֶׁר עַל הָאָרֶץ. כֹּל מַפְרֶסֶת פַּרְסָה וְשֹׁסַעַת
שֶׁסַע פְּרָסֹת מַעֲלַת גֵּרָה בַּבְּהֵמָה אֹתָהּ תֹּאכֵלוּ.

God spoke to Moshe and Aharon, telling them to speak to the Israelites, and convey the following to them:

Of all the animals in the world, these are the ones that you may eat: Among mammals, you may eat any one that has [true] hooves that are cloven and that brings up its cud.

Vayikra 11:1–3

EXERCISE 3

Which of the following animals is kosher?

A. Porcupine
B. Lamb
C. Cat
D. Rabbit

How about these?

A. Pig
B. Antelope
C. Horse
D. Donkey

Are any of these kosher?

A. Bison
B. Water Buffalo
C. Giraffe
D. Deer

KEY POINT

TEXT 3A

וְאֶת הַחֲזִיר כִּי מַפְרִיס פַּרְסָה הוּא וְשֹׁסַע שֶׁסַע
פַּרְסָה וְהוּא גֵּרָה לֹא יִגָּר טָמֵא הוּא לָכֶם.

The pig shall be [nonkosher] to you although it has a [true] hoof that is cloven, because it does not chew its cud. . . .

Vayikra 11:7

TEXT 3B

When the pig lies down, it extends its hooves, as if to say, "See, I am kosher!"

Rashi, Bereishit 26:34

EXERCISE 4

Which physical characteristics identify kosher varieties of fish?

A. Tail and fins

B. Fins and scales

C. Teeth and gills

D. Shell and claws

TEXT 4

אֶת זֶה תֹּאכְלוּ מִכֹּל אֲשֶׁר בַּמָּיִם כֹּל אֲשֶׁר לוֹ סְנַפִּיר וְקַשְׂקֶשֶׂת בַּמַּיִם בַּיַּמִּים וּבַנְּחָלִים אֹתָם תֹּאכֵלוּ. וְכֹל אֲשֶׁר אֵין לוֹ סְנַפִּיר וְקַשְׂקֶשֶׂת בַּיַּמִּים וּבַנְּחָלִים מִכֹּל שֶׁרֶץ הַמַּיִם וּמִכֹּל נֶפֶשׁ הַחַיָּה אֲשֶׁר בַּמָּיִם שֶׁקֶץ הֵם לָכֶם.

This is what you may eat of all that is in the water: You may eat any creature that lives in the water, whether in seas or rivers, as long as it has fins and scales. All creatures in seas and rivers that do not have fins and scales, whether they are small aquatic animals or other aquatic creatures, must be avoided by you.

Vayikra 11:9–10

KEY POINT

____

____

____

Which of the following aquatic species is kosher?

A. Dogfish

B. Catfish

C. Tuna

D. Shark

EXERCISE 6

Which of the following aquatic species is NOT kosher?

A. Barracuda

B. Salmon

C. Red Snapper

D. Swordfish

MIXED MESSAGES

TEXT 5

לֹא תְבַשֵּׁל גְּדִי בַּחֲלֵב אִמּוֹ.

Do not cook a kid [goat] in its mother's milk.

Shemot 23:19

KEY POINT

SOUL FOOD

TEXT 6

Know that these foods were not forbidden to us because of their effect on our body's health. . . . Were that so, it would have diminished the stature of the divine Torah, placing it at the level of those kinds of medical books that are short in their words and explanations. This would be disgraceful.

Besides, it would be possible to fix the harmful nature of these foods by adding various ingredients and mixtures that would nullify any damaging property, as we do with the deadly poisons that we transform into all kinds of healing medicines. Therefore, no prohibition should remain and the Torah would be like a fraud. . . .

QUESTION FOR DISCUSSION

According this text, what is the true reason for keeping kosher? What arguments are provided to support this idea?

Also we see that the non-Jews who are not careful about this and eat the meat of swine and other nonkosher animals, fowl, and fish live in good health and show no weakness or infirmity on this account.

Rather, they are prohibited because of their effect on the soul and its health. . . .

Rabbi Yitschak Arma'ah, *Akeidat Yitschak, Sha'ar* 60

FIGURE 2.1

Myth	Kosher food is held to a higher quality standard, and is healthier than nonkosher food.
Fact	

BEYOND REASON

TEXT 7

It is appropriate for one to meditate on the laws of the holy Torah, to know their purpose according to one's capacity. [However,] if one cannot find a reason or a rationale for a practice, one should not regard it lightly. . . .

The Torah states (Vayikra 19:37), "And you shall guard all of My *chukim* and all of My *mishpatim* and perform them." . . *Mishpatim* are *mitzvot* whose justifications are evident, and the practical benefits of their observance are known: for example, the prohibitions against robbery and bloodshed, and the commandment to honor one's father and mother.

Chukim are *mitzvot* whose reasons are not known, as our sages said, "[God says,] 'Observe My *chukim*, and you have no permission to question them'" (Talmud, Yoma 67a). A person naturally chafes against their observance, and the nations of the world challenge them, such as the prohibition of the meat of a pig, and [the mixture of] milk and meat. . . .

Maimonides, *Mishneh Torah*, Laws of Misappropriation of Sacred Property 8:8

QUESTION FOR DISCUSSION

Why would God give us *mitzvot* that we cannot fully understand? Why are *chukim* important?

KEY POINT

FIGURE 2.2

Word	Definition	Examples
Mishpatim		
Chukim		

KOSHER QUESTIONABLES

GLATT KOSHER

EXERCISE 7

A *glatt* kosher product is:

A. any food produced by an Orthodox Jewish company.

B. any food that meets a stricter set of kosher rules.

C. any food that is both kosher and organic.

D. none of the above.

TEXT 8A

וְאַנְשֵׁי קֹדֶשׁ תִּהְיוּן לִי, וּבָשָׂר בַּשָּׂדֶה טְרֵפָה לֹא תֹאכֵלוּ, לַכֶּלֶב תַּשְׁלִכוּן אֹתוֹ.

You shall be holy people unto Me; an animal that is a mauled in the field you shall not eat. . . .

Shemot 22:30

QUESTION FOR DISCUSSION

What is this verse forbidding?

KEY POINT

TEXT 8B

There is no difference between an animal that was attacked and battered by an animal, fell from the roof and broke the majority of its ribs, fell and crushed its limbs, was shot with an arrow that pierced its heart or lung, developed an illness that caused its heart or lung to be perforated, broke the majority of its ribs, or the like—because it is on the verge of death, regardless of the cause, it is a *tereifah*. . . .

Maimonides, *Mishneh Torah*, Laws of Forbidden Foods 4:8

FIGURE 2.3

Myth	*Glatt* kosher means extra kosher.
Fact	

WHAT IS KOSHER SALT?

TEXT 9

וְאֹמַר לִבְנֵי יִשְׂרָאֵל, "דַּם כָּל בָּשָׂר לֹא תֹאכֵלוּ".

And I say to the Children of Israel, "You shall not eat the blood of any flesh."

Vayikra 17:14

TEXT 10

One should not use salt that is fine like flour, nor salt that is exceedingly coarse that rolls off the meat.

Rabbi Yosef Caro, *Shulchan Aruch*, *Yoreh De'ah* 69:3

KEY POINT

FOOD STRUGGLES

KEY POINT

QUESTION FOR DISCUSSION

How does this interpretation differ from the simple understanding of the biblical story?

TEXT 11A

One who desires bread should eat it with the blade of a sword.

Zohar 3:188b

TEXT 11B

The time of eating is a time of battle.

Zohar 3:272a

TEXT 12

All the trees in the garden possessed the potential of both the Tree of Life and the Tree of Knowledge of Good and Evil. . . . Had Adam eaten from "the Tree of Life"—that is, had he eaten properly, and not merely to indulge his body—he would have experienced the holiness of the Tree of Life in his eating. . . . But because he ate from the Tree of Knowledge, that is, with the awareness of his sensory pleasure, all subsequent eating was tainted with the desire for bodily gratification.

Rabbi Tsadok Hakohen Rabinowitz, *Peri Tsadik, Parashat Bereishit* 8

TEXT 13

"You shall be holy people unto Me." The Rebbe of Kotsk said: This is what God is saying: "I have enough angels without you, I have no need for you to be angelic. Instead, 'you shall be holy *people* unto Me.' Be human, live as human beings do—but be holy human beings, a holy people.'"

Rabbi Shlomo Yosef Zevin, *LeTorah Ulemo'adim,* Shemot 25:2

KEY POINT

TEXT 14

The object of all these laws [concerning forbidden food] is to restrain the growth of desire, the indulgence in seeking that which is pleasant, and the disposition to consider the appetite for eating and drinking as the purpose of a person's existence.

Maimonides, *Guide for the Perplexed* 3:35

KEY POINT

____

____

TEXT 15

It is forbidden to enjoy anything of this world without reciting a blessing. . . . To enjoy anything of this world without a blessing is like making personal use of things consecrated to heaven, because it says, "The earth and all that is in it belong to God" (Tehilim 24:1).

Talmud, Berachot 35a

NOTE

If you've said the blessing over bread, all other foods and drinks (other than wine) in that meal are included. There are also blessings recited when we finish eating, wherein we thank God for the food we have eaten. Refer to a prayer book for the texts of those blessings.

FIGURE 2.4

All food blessings begin with the same words:

בָּרוּךְ אַתָּה ה' אֱלֹקֵינוּ מֶלֶךְ הָעוֹלָם . . .	Blessed are You, Lord our God, King of the Universe . . .

The concluding words depend on the food you are eating:

For fruit of a tree	
. . . בּוֹרֵא פְּרִי הָעֵץ	". . . Who creates the fruit of the tree."

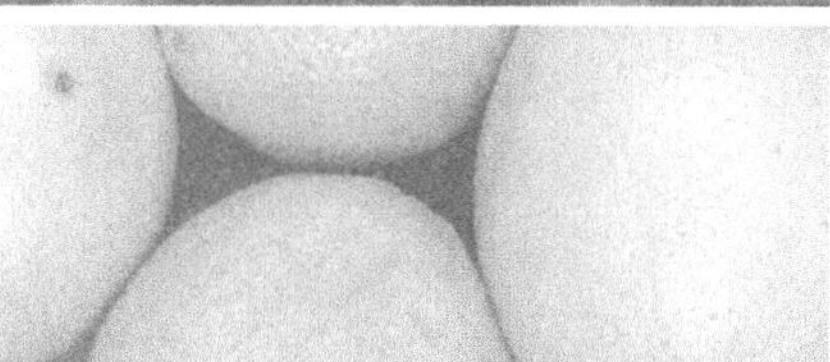

For a vegetable or fruit of a plant	
... בּוֹרֵא פְּרִי הָאֲדָמָה	"... Who creates the fruit of the earth."
For food made from wheat, barley, oat, spelt, or rye (besides bread)	
... בּוֹרֵא מִינֵי מְזוֹנוֹת	"... Who creates various kinds of foods."
For bread or matzah	
... הַמּוֹצִיא לֶחֶם מִן הָאָרֶץ	"... Who brings forth bread from the earth."
For wine or grape juice	
... בּוֹרֵא פְּרִי הַגָּפֶן	"... Who creates the fruit of the vine."
For everything else, e.g., dairy, meat, beverages	
... שֶׁהַכֹּל נִהְיָה בִּדְבָרוֹ	"... by Whose word all things came to be."

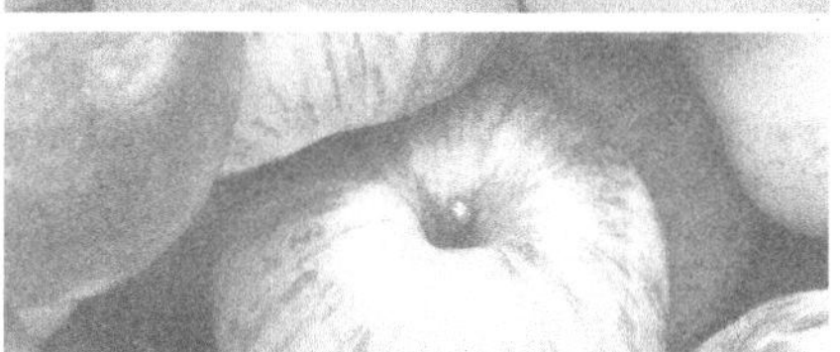

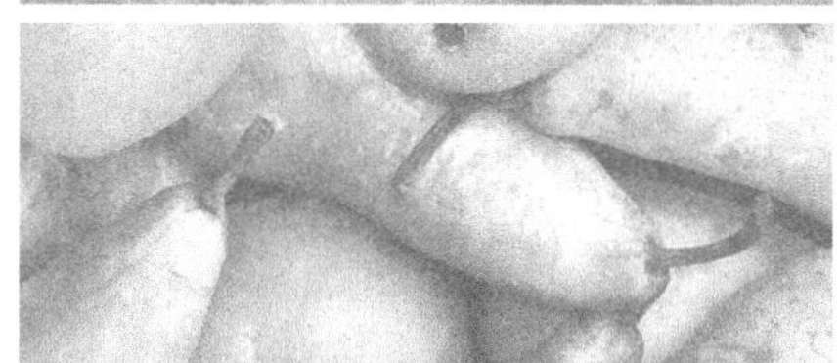

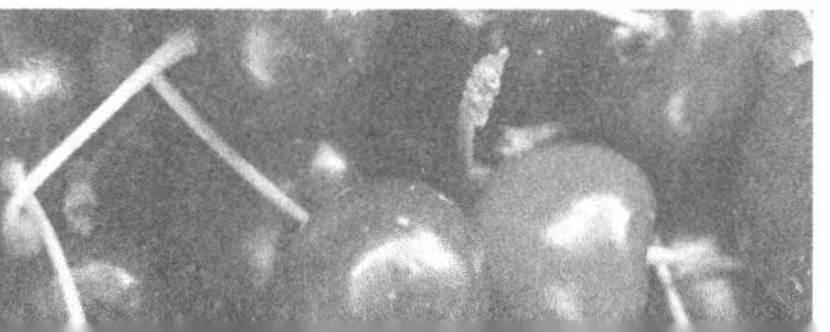

Lesson Three

BODY TABOOS

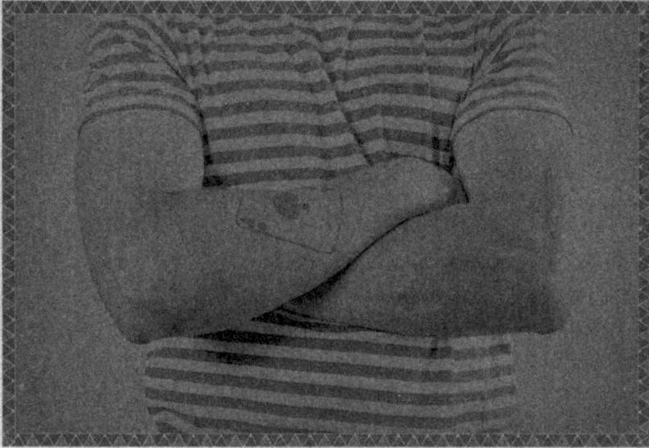

MYTHBUSTERS

JEWS AND TATTOOS

THE MARK OF A MYTH

CASE STUDY 1

In the TV series, "*Curb Your Enthusiasm*" (HBO), there was an episode where Larry David's mother was buried in a special section of the Jewish cemetery "reserved for people who just don't qualify for interment in consecrated ground" because of a small tattoo that she had on her body. The manager of the cemetery explained to a distraught David that "to adorn oneself in such a manner, was found by Maimonides—many, many, years ago, of course—to be an offense that would disqualify such a person from burial in consecrated ground." Despite David's pleas, the manager asserted that he could do nothing to help him, because "the law is the law." So, under the cover of darkness and after some bribes, David and some family members dug up his mother's body to bury her in the regular section of the Jewish cemetery.

TEXT 1

וְשֶׂרֶט לָנֶפֶשׁ לֹא תִתְּנוּ בִּבְשַׂרְכֶם, וּכְתֹבֶת קַעֲקַע לֹא תִתְּנוּ בָּכֶם, אֲנִי ה'.

You shall not make cuts in your flesh for a person [who died]. You shall not etch a tattoo on yourselves. I am the Lord.

Vayikra 19:28

KEY POINT

EXERCISE 1

Which of the following activities is prohibited because of its similarity to tattooing?

A. Doodling on your palm with a ballpoint pen

B. Dying your hair electric blue

C. Decorating your hands and feet at a bridal henna party

D. None of the above

QUESTION FOR DISCUSSION

Would this procedure be allowed under Jewish law?

CASE STUDY 2

Recently, procedures have been developed for women to apply permanent or semipermanent makeup. In the process of applying permanent makeup, a needle deposits colored pigments made from iron oxide into the skin's dermal layer. This procedure is applied on the lips and/or around the eyes and can be either permanent or semipermanent.

FIGURE 3.1

Myth	Jews with tattoos cannot be buried in a Jewish cemetery.
Fact	

THAT SPECIAL GIFT

TEXT 2

It was the custom of the heathens to brand themselves for their deity, thereby demonstrating that they are servants branded for its service.

Sefer Hachinuch, Mitzvah 253

QUESTIONS FOR DISCUSSION

Is it necessary to abstain from getting a tattoo if it doesn't have any religious significance to you? Would it be okay to get a Jewish tattoo, such as a Star of David, that cannot possibly be mistaken as pagan or idolatrous?

CASE STUDY 3

One of the characters in Shakespeare's famous play, *The Merchant of Venice*, is a Jewish moneylender named Shylock, who demands that a Venetian gentile merchant named Antonio give Shylock a pound of his flesh for defaulting on a loan for which Antonio served as a guarantor. The plot concludes with a climactic courtroom drama in which Shylock's demands are defeated by the deft arguments of the defendant's lawyer.

QUESTION FOR DISCUSSION

Can you think of any halachic problems with the notion that Shylock would demand "a pound of flesh" as repayment for a loan?

KEY POINT

TEXT 3

A person's life and body do not belong to him. Not only is it forbidden for a person to destroy his life, in whole or in part, but also his life does not belong to him in the first place. If he sells, gives away, or gives in pledge the flesh of his body to be chopped or sliced, it is as if he had given away something that was not his. The transaction is invalid. "God gives and God takes away" (Iyov 1:21) is not just a comforting cliché but a definition of reality. . . .

According to Jewish law, the agreement between Shylock and Antonio is null and void from the start, even if extracting a slice of living flesh would not endanger the life of the giver; how much the more so when there is no assurance that it would not result in death.

[As expressed in Jewish prayer,] "The soul is Yours and the body is Your handiwork; the soul is Yours and the body is Yours–the property of the blessed Holy One!"

Rabbi Shlomo Yosef Zevin, *Le'or HaHalachah,* "The Case of Shylock in Light of Jewish Law"

TEXT 4

It is forbidden to hit another person, even with the other person's consent. A person has no authority over his body to grant permission that it be struck, denigrated, or pained.

Rabbi Shne'ur Zalman of Liadi, *Shulchan Aruch HaRav, Choshen Mishpat, Hilchot Nizkei Guf Vanefesh 4*

TEXT 5

וְנִשְׁמַרְתֶּם מְאֹד לְנַפְשֹׁתֵיכֶם.

And you shall watch yourselves very well!

Devarim 4:15

KEY POINT

___

___

___

___

PLASTIC SURGERY

QUESTION FOR DISCUSSION

What would Jewish law say about tampering with one's body for cosmetic purposes?

TEXT 6

When then-17-year-old Kylie Jenner admitted to getting lip fillers, it caused expressions of shock–and even anger–across the Internet. But the fact is, she's just one of thousands of teenagers who are undergoing cosmetic procedures.

According to the American Society of Plastic Surgeons, nearly 64,000 cosmetic surgery patients in 2014 were aged 13–19, and experts believe this number is bound to rise.

"There has been an increase in teens coming in for plastic surgery," Dr. Richard Ellenbogen, CEO of Beverly Hills Body, tells PEOPLE Magazine. "This is directly related to the surgery of the stars of their reality shows, and the acceptance of cosmetic procedures on social media."

Gabrielle Olya, "The Newest Back-to-School Must-Have for Teens? Cosmetic Surgery," August 28, 2015, www.People.com

TEXT 7

It is forbidden for a person to injure himself or another. Not only a person who causes an injury, but anyone who strikes another person . . . with malice violates a biblical prohibition.

Maimonides, *Mishneh Torah*, Laws of Injury and Damages 5:1

QUESTION FOR DISCUSSION

How is this passage from Maimonides' code instructive in regard to the issue of plastic surgery?

FIGURE 3.2

Myth	Jewish law prohibits cosmetic surgery.
Fact	

SACRED ACTS

RESPECT THE BODY

EXERCISE 2

What are some ways in which you see people not showing proper respect to their own bodies?

___

___

What are some things that you already do to take care of your body? How can you give your body even greater care?

___

___

How can your body be used to cause harm and destruction? How can it be used to make the world more beautiful?

___

___

FIGURE 3.3

Myth	Judaism regards the physical body as an obstacle to holiness.
Fact	

A MICROCOSMIC TEMPLE

TEXT 8

When the Jews came up [to Jerusalem] for the festivals, they would roll aside the curtain [that separated the people from the Holy of Holies], and the *cherubim*—whose bodies were intertwined one with another—were shown to them. And the assembled Jews would be told, "Look! You are beloved before God as the love between man and woman."

Talmud, Yoma 54a

QUESTION FOR DISCUSSION

Why was this imagery present in the Temple?

KEY POINT

____

____

____

____

____

TEXT 9

God only abides and dwells "in one," in the person who achieves a holy oneness—nowhere else.

When is a person called "one"? . . . When a person is in the union of marital intimacy. . . . When husband and wife join, they become one. They are one in body and one in soul; they are one person. And God dwells in the oneness.

Zohar 3:80a–b

TEXT 10

Marital intimacy, when properly experienced, is great and sublime. It shares the profound secret of the cherubim, which were in the form of a male and female intertwined with each other.

If it were shameful, God would not have commanded [the Jewish people] to fashion the cherubim and place them in the holiest and purest place in the world!

Rabbi Moshe ben Nachman, *Igeret Hakodesh*

HOLY WHAT?

TEXT 11

A husband may not treat [his wife] in the manner of the Persians, who have marital intimacy while clothed. . . . Saying, "I can only [engage in marital intimacy] while I wear my clothes and my wife wears hers," is grounds for divorce.

Talmud, Ketubot 48a

KEY POINT

FIGURE 3.4

Myth	Orthodox couples are supposed to have marital intimacy through a hole in a sheet.
Fact	

Lesson Four

LIFE AFTER LIFE

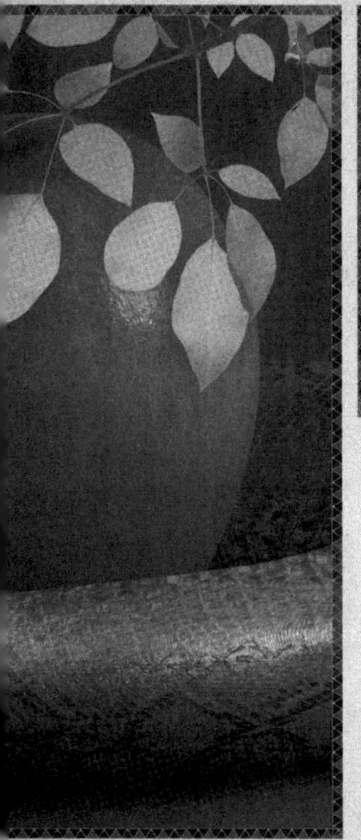

MythBUSTERS

DEATH: END OR BEGINNING?

THE VIEW FROM ABOVE

QUESTION FOR DISCUSSION

What do you think happens after we die? Do you believe that there is life after death?

TEXT 1

Death is a depressingly inevitable consequence of life, but now scientists believe they may have found some light at the end of the tunnel.

The largest ever medical study into near-death and out-of-body experiences has discovered that some awareness may continue even after the brain has shut down completely. It is a controversial subject which has, until recently, been treated with widespread skepticism.

But scientists at the University of Southampton have spent four years examining more than 2,000 people who suffered cardiac arrests at 15 hospitals in the UK, US and Austria. And they found that nearly 40 percent of people who survived described some kind of "awareness" during the time when they were clinically dead before their hearts were restarted.

One man even recalled leaving his body entirely and watching his resuscitation from the corner of the room. Despite being unconscious and "dead" for three minutes, the 57-year-old social worker from Southampton recounted the actions of the nursing staff in detail and described the sound of the machines.

"We know the brain can't function when the heart has stopped beating," said Dr. Sam Parnia, a former research fellow at Southampton University, now at the State University of New York, who led the study. "But in this case, conscious awareness appears to have continued for up to three minutes into the period when the heart wasn't beating, even though the brain typically shuts down within 20–30 seconds after the heart has stopped. . . ."

. . . Dr. Parnia believes many more people may have experiences when they are close to death but drugs or sedatives used in the process of resuscitation may stop them [from] remembering.

"Many people have assumed that these were hallucinations or illusions, but they do seem to correspond to actual events. And a higher proportion of people may have vivid death experiences, but do not recall them due to the effects of brain injury or sedative drugs on memory circuits. These experiences warrant further investigation."

Sarah Knapton, "First Hint of 'Life After Death' in Biggest Ever Scientific Study," www.telegraph.co.uk, Oct. 7, 2014

KEY POINT

BORN TWICE

TEXT 2A

כִּי עָפָר אַתָּה וְאֶל עָפָר תָּשׁוּב

For dust you are and to dust you will return.

Bereishit 3:19

TEXT 2B

וְיָשֹׁב הֶעָפָר עַל הָאָרֶץ כְּשֶׁהָיָה וְהָרוּחַ תָּשׁוּב אֶל הָאֱלֹהִים אֲשֶׁר נְתָנָהּ

The dust returns to the dust as it was, but the spirit returns to God who gave it.

Kohelet 12:7

QUESTIONS FOR DISCUSSION

What do these texts communicate about what happens to us at the end of life? Are they contradictory or complementary?

TEXT 3

The form of this soul is not a combination of the physical elements, into which it will ultimately decompose. . . . Rather, it is from God, from Heaven.

Therefore, when the matter of the body, which is a combination of [physical] elements, decomposes . . . this soul does not cease to be. . . . Rather, it exists forever.

Maimonides, *Mishneh Torah*, Laws of the Fundamentals of the Torah 4:9

KEY POINT

TEXT 4

Life is real! Life is earnest!

And the grave is not its goal;

Dust thou art, to dust returnest,

Was not spoken of the soul.

Excerpt from "A Psalm of Life," (1839) Henry Wadsworth Longfellow, American poet and social activist

KEY POINT

EXERCISE 1

1. The same Hebrew word is used for "womb" and "grave." What does this indicate about the Jewish view of the afterlife?
2. What is the skeptic's argument? Can you identify with the skeptic? Please explain your answer.
3. What is the believer's argument? Can you identify with the believer? Please explain your answer.
4. Why is it so hard for the skeptic and believer to come to an agreement?

THE AFTERLIFE

HEAVEN: CLOSE FOR COMFORT

TEXT 5

The concept of spiritual reward is abstruse and difficult for human intellect (while still attached to the physical body) to visualize and grasp. Just as the blind person cannot grasp the concept of colors, so too, the spirit, while still engaged with the physical, cannot grasp purely spiritual matters.

Don Yitschak Abarbanel, Vayikra 26:3–46

KEY POINT

TEXT 6

In the hereafter there is no eating, drinking, procreation, commerce, jealousy, hatred, or competition. Rather, the righteous sit, their heads adorned by crowns, and they delight in the radiance of the Divine Presence.

Talmud, Berachot 17a

KEY POINT

EXERCISE 2

Rate the following things in terms of how pleasurable they are (1 = least pleasurable; 10 = most pleasurable).

A Hawaiian cruise

1 2 3 4 5 6 7 8 9 10

A lifetime of meaning

1 2 3 4 5 6 7 8 9 10

True love

1 2 3 4 5 6 7 8 9 10

Being very popular

1 2 3 4 5 6 7 8 9 10

Potato chips

1 2 3 4 5 6 7 8 9 10

Wealth

1 2 3 4 5 6 7 8 9 10

Wisdom

1 2 3 4 5 6 7 8 9 10

TEXT 7

Rabbi Ya'akov would say: This world is comparable to the antechamber before the World to Come. Prepare yourself in the antechamber, so that you may enter the banquet hall. . . . And a single moment of bliss in the World to Come is greater than all of the [pleasure found in the] present [physical] world.

Mishnah, Avot 4:16-17

KEY POINT

____

____

____

____

____

FIGURE 4.1

Myth	Heaven is a dreamlike place in the sky where angels and souls frolic among the clouds.
Fact	

A LIFE OF CONSEQUENCE

TEXT 8

The eleventh principle:

That God, blessed be He, gives reward to those who observe the commandments of the Torah and punishes those who transgress its prohibitions.

Maimonides, *Commentary on the Mishnah*, Introduction to *Perek Chelek*

TEXT 9

The punishments described in the Torah are not similar to the punishments meted for transgressing the decree of an earthly king. Rather, the Torah's punishments are natural consequences. One who fails to observe a Torah commandment is denied the good that naturally results from its observance. This is similar to one who doesn't sow, who then, obviously, cannot reap; or one who doesn't wear clothing and then becomes cold; or the nature of fire to cause heat; the nature of water to make wet; and the nature of bread to satiate. Similarly, it is the nature of each mitzvah to elicit the positive consequences that are promised for its observance or the negative consequences for its transgression.

Rabbi Menachem Recanati, Shemot 29:1

EXERCISE 3

We all need food to survive. When it comes to obtaining food, there are two possible ways to go about it. Which one best compares to the way that we receive reward for the *mitzvot* that we do?

1. A business person (or tailor, janitor, etc.) works for a living. In exchange for his work he receives money, with which he purchases food.
2. A farmer sows his fields with seeds and then reaps the produce.

KEY POINT

FIGURE 4.2

Profession	Process
Businessperson	Work – Money – Food
Farmer	Sow – Reap – Food

TEXT 10

The reward of a mitzvah is a mitzvah; the retribution for a sin is a sin.

Mishnah, Avot 4:2

QUESTIONS FOR DISCUSSION

What does this story illustrate regarding the consequences of our actions? What do the precious stones represent? What do the fish represent?

TEXT 11

Once upon a time there was a poor man who heard that in a faraway land, on the other side of the deep and dangerous sea, there was a place where diamonds were as plentiful as dust–one need only bend down, scoop them up, and fill one's pockets.

After a long and arduous journey, the man arrived in this wondrous land. Everything that had been said about it was true! Diamonds of all sizes were strewn everywhere: even the sand was comprised of billions of tiny glittering gems. A group of children gathered to watch the strange visitor kneeling on the ground and stuffing his pockets with stones and pebbles, but the man was too busy to notice them. They started to point and jeer at him, "What are you doing, silly man?"

He quickly learned that these pebbles, each of which would be worth millions back home, were utterly worthless on the island because they were so abundant. Instead, the currency with which people paid for goods and services was fish. In fact, few people remembered that fish were originally consumed as a food. No one was bothered by the stench that emanated from their wallets, pocketbooks, and money closets. Indeed, a reeking establishment exuded the sweet aura of old money.

Once he overcame his initial disappointment, the traveler set his mind to the task of amassing a wealth of fish. He was a most resourceful and ambitious individual. He worked hard, invested wisely, and before long he was one of the wealthiest people in the land. His businesses were headquartered in the most rancid section of old downtown, and his private vaults held thousands of tons of fish.

Finally, it was time to return home. He telegraphed his family, "I am rich. We shall never want for anything in our lives. Prepare for my triumphant homecoming." He loaded his fortune on a fleet of ships, and set sail for his hometown.

Family and friends, dressed in their best, awaited him eagerly at the seaport. To his dismay, the customs officials deemed his putrid cargo a hazard to public health, and refused him entry until he got rid of it. There was nothing that could be done with his shiploads of rotted fish except sail back a few miles from shore and dump them into the sea.

But later that day, as he was undressing for bed, a few tiny gems were shaken out of his trouser pockets and sparkled on the floor of his home. He and his family never again wanted for anything in their lives.

Adapted from an article by Rabbi Yanki Tauber, "Diamonds and Fish," Chabad.org

HELL: SOUL CLEANSE

QUESTION FOR DISCUSSION

Why was it better for Acher to be judged in *Gehinom*?

TEXT 12

When Acher died, the heavenly court declared: "Let him not be judged [in *Gehinom*] for his sins, nor let him enter Paradise." [Their reasoning was:] Let him not be judged, because he engaged in Torah study, nor let him enter Paradise, because he [so egregiously] sinned.

[Acher's former disciple] Rabbi Meir said: "Better that he be judged and then enter Paradise."

Talmud, Chagigah 15b

KEY POINT

____

____

____

____

____

TEXT 13

The purpose of *Gehinom* is to refine the soul and rid it of any negativity that it contracted. This is similar to the process of smelting silver, wherein the dross is burned away in a furnace, leaving the silver clean and without impurities. So, too, for the soul to be able to process the supernal pleasures, for it to be able to take delight [in God's radiance], it must first be refined in the "fires" of *Gehinom,* wherein the good is separated from the bad.

Rabbi Shne'ur Zalman of Liadi, *Torah Or* 49b

SENTENCING GUIDELINES

TEXT 14

All of Israel has a portion in the World to Come, as it is stated (Yeshayahu 60:21), "Your people are all righteous; they shall inherit the land forever; they are the branch of My planting, the work of My hands, in which [I] take pride."

Mishnah, Sanhedrin 10:1

TEXT 15

The wicked are judged in *Gehinom* for [a maximum of] twelve months.

Mishnah, Eduyot 2:10

KEY POINT

FIGURE 4.3

Myth	Hell is a place where souls are punished with eternal damnation for their sins.
Fact	

TRUE PURPOSE

FIGURE 4.4

Myth	Judaism says that our ultimate purpose in life is to do good deeds in order to attain bliss in the afterlife.
Fact	

EXERCISE 4

Imagine for a moment a medical researcher who spends many years in the lab, and finally succeeds in finding a cure for all cancers. With this one discovery, all of the suffering and pain of millions of people is removed from the face of the earth.

The Nobel Prize committee hears of the discovery, and waits to confirm that this dreaded disease has been eradicated, and that in fact, this is a discovery worthy of the highest honor in the field of medicine. Eventually, an invitation is extended to the researcher to come to Sweden with family and friends to receive the coveted award at a magnificent ceremony.

Now place yourself in the shoes of this medical researcher. Would the Nobel Prize be your proudest achievement? What other reward might be more meaningful?

KEY POINT

____

____

____

____

____

TEXT 16

[Rabbi Ya'akov] would also say: A single moment of repentance and good deeds in this world is greater than all of the World to Come.

Mishnah, Avot 4:17

KEY POINT

TEXT 17

The primary reward in the hereafter is the soul returning to its Source and uniting with God. Certainly, however, it is even greater when the soul can connect with God *here in this world* [through the study of Torah and the performance of *mitzvot*], for that is the purpose of Creation.

Rabbi Eliyahu of Vilna, Commentary on *Shir Hashirim* 1:3

TEXT 18

When our master and teacher [Rabbi Shne'ur Zalman of Liadi] would enter a state of spiritual ecstasy, he would be heard exclaiming:

"I want nothing at all! I don't want Your Heaven, I don't want Your World to Come. . . . I want nothing but You alone."

Rabbi Menachem Mendel of Lubavitch, *Derech Mitsvotecha* 138a

Lesson Five

FANTASTICAL FORCES

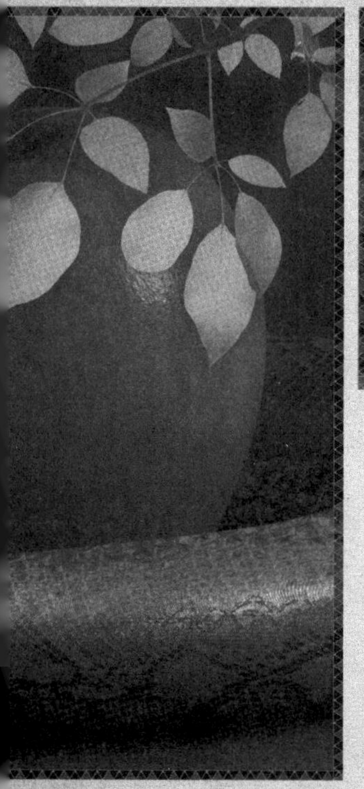

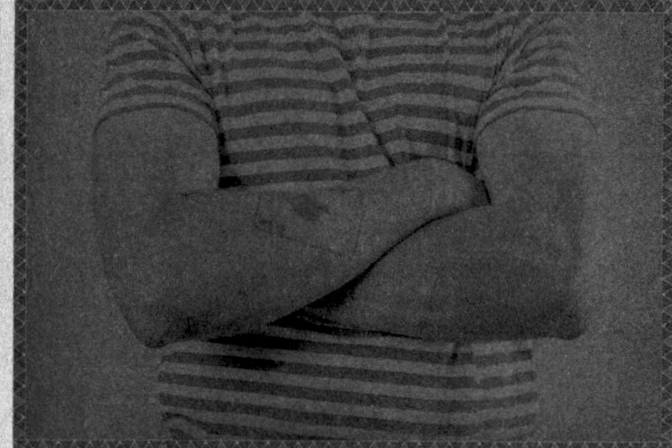

MythBUSTERS

MYTHICAL OR MYSTICAL?

1 = Definitely Not
2 = Probably Not
3 = Not Sure
4 = Probably Yes
5 = Definitely Yes

EXERCISE 1

Circle the number that best describes your belief.

A. Is there such a thing as a "Force" that impacts physical reality?

1 2 3 4 5

B. Can people be harmed by an "evil eye"?

1 2 3 4 5

C. Do people have guardian angels?

1 2 3 4 5

D. Does the Devil or Satan exist?

1 2 3 4 5

TEXT 1

According to a 2005 Gallup poll, three out of four Americans profess at least one paranormal belief.

David W. Moore, *Three in Four Americans Believe in Paranormal*, www.gallup.com, June 16, 2005

KEY POINT

REACHING FOR ANGELS

FIGURE 5.1

Myth	Judaism does not discuss the supernatural.
Fact	

QUESTION FOR DISCUSSION

How is the angel described in this text depicted differently from an angel that you might find on a Hallmark card?

TEXT 2A

וְאַרְבָּעָה פָנִים לְאֶחָד פְּנֵי הָאֶחָד פְּנֵי הַכְּרוּב וּפְנֵי הַשֵּׁנִי
פְּנֵי אָדָם וְהַשְּׁלִישִׁי פְּנֵי אַרְיֵה וְהָרְבִיעִי פְּנֵי נָשֶׁר...

אַרְבָּעָה אַרְבָּעָה פָנִים לְאֶחָד וְאַרְבַּע כְּנָפַיִם לְאֶחָד
וּדְמוּת יְדֵי אָדָם תַּחַת כַּנְפֵיהֶם

Now each [angel] had four faces: the face of one was the face of the [angelic] cherub, and the face of the second was the face of a man, and the third the face of a lion, and the fourth the face of an eagle. . . .

Four faces each for every one, and four wings for every one, and the likeness of the hands of a man was beneath their wings.

Yechezkel 10:14, 21

TEXT 2B

בִּשְׁנַת מוֹת הַמֶּלֶךְ עֻזִּיָּהוּ וָאֶרְאֶה אֶת אֲדֹנָי יֹשֵׁב עַל כִּסֵּא רָם וְנִשָּׂא ...

שְׂרָפִים עֹמְדִים מִמַּעַל לוֹ שֵׁשׁ כְּנָפַיִם שֵׁשׁ כְּנָפַיִם לְאֶחָד
בִּשְׁתַּיִם | יְכַסֶּה פָנָיו וּבִשְׁתַּיִם יְכַסֶּה רַגְלָיו וּבִשְׁתַּיִם יְעוֹפֵף

וְקָרָא זֶה אֶל זֶה וְאָמַר קָדוֹשׁ | קָדוֹשׁ קָדוֹשׁ
יְהוָה צְבָאוֹת מְלֹא כָל הָאָרֶץ כְּבוֹדוֹ

In the year of the death of King Uzziah, I saw [a prophetic image of] the Lord sitting on a high and exalted throne...

Seraphim stood above Him, six wings, six wings to each one; with two he would cover his face, and with two he would cover his feet, and with two he would fly.

And one called to the other and said, "Holy, holy, holy is the Lord of Hosts; the whole Earth is full of His glory."

Yeshayahu 6:1–3

QUESTION FOR DISCUSSION

What insights can we learn from the above texts regarding angels?

FIGURE 5.2

Myth	Angels look like people with wings on their backs and halos above their heads.
Fact	

HOW ANGELS ROLL

SPIRITUAL ROBOTS

TEXT 3

One who does one mitzvah is given one angel. One who does two *mitzvot* is given two angels. One who does all of the *mitzvot* is given many angels, as it says, "For His angels He will assign to you" (Tehilim 91:11). And what is the function of these angels? They guard the person against harm.

Midrash, *Tanchuma* (Warsaw edition), Mishpatim 19

TEXT 4

The essence of the commandment [forbidding] idolatry is the prohibition against worshipping any of the creations: not an angel, sphere, or star, none of the four fundamental elements, nor any entity created from them. This is true even if the worshipper acknowledges that God is the [ultimate] authority.

Maimonides, *Mishneh Torah,* Laws of Idolatry 2:1

KEY POINT

____

____

____

____

____

FIGURE 5.3

Myth	Angels are supposed to answer our prayers for protection from harm.
Fact	

ANGELS VS. HUMAN BEINGS

QUESTION FOR DISCUSSION

Why do angels regard the physical world as so much more precious than the upper worlds?

TEXT 5

In the upper worlds, the preciousness of this world is well appreciated. The ministering angels. . .would forego everything for one *"Amen, yehei shemeih raba"* said by a Jew with full concentration, i.e., with total focus on the words.

Rabbi Shne'ur Zalman of Liadi, cited in *Hayom Yom,* 17 Adar I

FIGURE 5.4

Myth	Angels are spiritually superior to human beings.
Fact	

FALLEN ANGELS

EXERCISE 2: DEVIL OR ADVOCATE?

Circle the answer that you find most accurate.

Satan is:

A. the archenemy of God.

B. a fallen angel who sinned and was punished.

C. a devoted angel who is doing exactly what he is meant to do.

D. nonexistent in the Jewish tradition.

FIGURE 5.5

Myth	Satan is the archenemy of God.
Fact	

EVIL EYE: THE DARK SIDE OF THE FORCE?

GOOD EYE VS. EVIL EYE

QUESTION FOR DISCUSSION

Why should viewing another with a good eye draw blessing upon his friend and upon himself as well?

TEXT 6

When one views another with a good eye, he blesses and draws beneficence upon his friend, and he too is blessed. The same is true in the converse. As it is stated (Mishlei 22:9), "One with a good eye shall be blessed," and [using alternate vowelization it can be] read, "[one with a good eye] shall bless."

Rabbi Elazar Ezkari, *Sefer Chareidim* 66:90

TEXT 7

May it be Your will, God, my God, and God of my fathers, to protect me this day and every day. . .from an evil eye.

Sidur Tehilat Hashem, Morning Blessings

KEY POINT

TEXT 8A

It is forbidden to stand near another's field when its crop is fully grown.

Talmud, Bava Metsia 107a

QUESTION FOR DISCUSSION

What could possibly be wrong with observing someone else's success?

KEY POINT

TEXT 8B

[Technically] two brothers or a father and son can be called up to receive consecutive *aliyot*. This is not done, however, to prevent the evil eye.

Rabbi Yosef Caro, *Shulchan Aruch*, *Orach Chayim* 142:6

KEY POINT

TEXT 9

One who speaks in praise of another—regarding his wisdom, wealth, children, and so forth—should also bless him, so that he not be affected by the evil eye.

Rabbi Chaim Yosef David Azulai, *Tsiporen Shamir* 172

DEFENSE AGAINST THE EVIL EYE

MODESTY

TEXT 10

Blessing is only found . . . in something hidden from sight.

Talmud, Ta'anit 8b

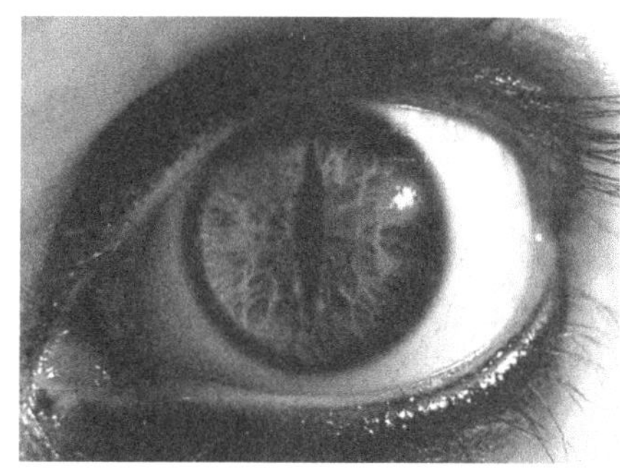

A GOOD EYE

TEXT 11

One who is generous and possessed of a good eye is not affected by the evil eye.

Rabbi Chaim Yosef David Azulai, *Devash Lefi, Ma'arechet Ayin, Erech Ayin Tovah*

MITZVAH PERFORMANCE

TEXT 12

One should not abstain from performing a mitzvah for fear of incurring the evil eye, for example, to invite a pauper into his home or to teach in public, to share the knowledge [of Torah] with the populace. For "one who observes the command will know no evil" (Kohelet 8:5); the mitzvah protects, it is a shield and armor.

Rabbi Eliezer Papo, *Peleh Yo'ets,* entry *Ayin Hara*

DON'T WORRY!

TEXT 13

With regard to the evil eye, while it is certainly a matter to consider, one mustn't be overly concerned. For regarding all such matters, the general principle is: "One who is not troubled by it, will not be troubled by it."

Rabbi Moshe Feinstein, *Sha'alot U'teshuvot Igrot Moshe, Even Ha'ezer* 3:26

TEXT 14

Know what is above you.

Mishnah, Avot 2:1

TEXT 15

This means to say: Know that all that is above is dependent on you.

Rabbi Dov Ber of Mezeritch, *Magid Devarav leYa'akov: Likutei Amarim* 198

KEY POINT

FIGURE 5.6

Myth	Judaism teaches that one should wear a red string to ward off the evil eye.
Fact	

Lesson Six

THE MESSIAH MYSTERY

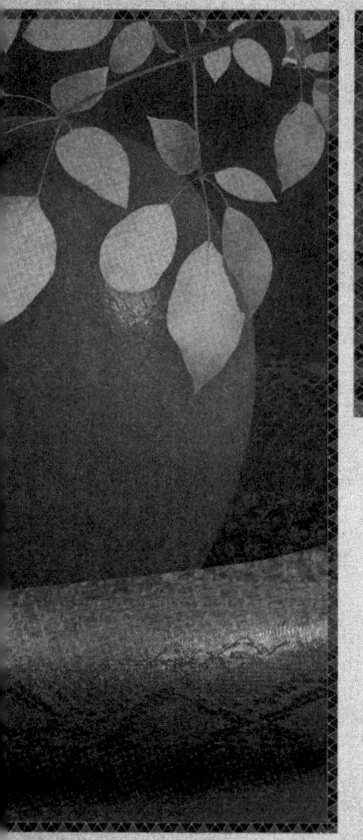

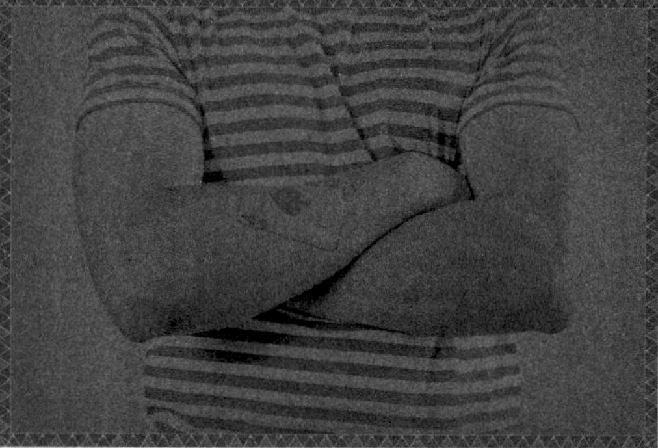

MythBUSTERS

DESTINY OR DELUSION?

QUESTION FOR DISCUSSION

What is Homer Simpson talking about when he proclaims himself to be the "Messiah"?

TEXT 1

mes·si·ah: noun

1. the promised deliverer of the Jewish nation prophesied in the Hebrew Bible.

2. a leader or savior of a particular group or cause.

"Messiah," Oxford Online Dictionaries [Oxford University Press, 2016]

TEXT 2A

וְשָׁב יְהֹוָה אֱלֹהֶיךָ אֶת שְׁבוּתְךָ וְרִחֲמֶךָ וְשָׁב וְקִבֶּצְךָ מִכָּל
הָעַמִּים אֲשֶׁר הֱפִיצְךָ יְהֹוָה אֱלֹהֶיךָ שָׁמָּה.

אִם יִהְיֶה נִדַּחֲךָ בִּקְצֵה הַשָּׁמָיִם מִשָּׁם יְקַבֶּצְךָ יְהֹוָה אֱלֹהֶיךָ וּמִשָּׁם יִקָּחֶךָ

וֶהֱבִיאֲךָ יְהֹוָה אֱלֹהֶיךָ אֶל הָאָרֶץ אֲשֶׁר יָרְשׁוּ אֲבֹתֶיךָ
וִירִשְׁתָּהּ וְהֵיטִבְךָ וְהִרְבְּךָ מֵאֲבֹתֶיךָ:

God will bring back your captivity and have mercy upon you. He will again gather you from among the nations. . . . Even if your Diaspora is at the ends of the heavens, God will gather you up from there... and bring you to the land....

Devarim 30:3–5

TEXT 2B

The Mashiach will appear one day and renew the Davidic dynasty and restore its sovereignty. He will build the Temple and gather the dispersed of Israel. At that time, we will observe all the *mitzvot* [related to the Temple and the Holy Land] as we did in days of yore....

One who does not believe in this redemption or does not await its coming denies not only the statements of the prophets [who spoke of the redemption], but also the words of the Torah and our teacher Moshe.

Maimonides, *Mishneh Torah*, Laws of Kings 11:1

KEY POINT

KEY POINT

____

____

____

____

____

FIGURE 6.1

THE THIRTEEN PRINCIPLES OF JEWISH FAITH

1. Belief in the existence of the Creator.
2. The belief that God is one.
3. The belief that God is not physical.
4. The belief in God's eternity–He always was, is, and will be.
5. The imperative to worship God exclusively and not any foreign false gods.
6. The belief that God communicates with man through prophecy.
7. The belief that the prophecy of Moshe, our teacher, is (and will always be) unequaled.
8. The belief in the divine origin of the Torah.
9. The belief that the Torah cannot be changed.
10. The belief in God's omniscience and providence.
11. The belief in divine reward and retribution.
12. The belief in the coming of Mashiach.
13. *To be announced! (____________________________)*

FIGURE 6.2

Myth	Mashiach is not a Jewish idea.
Fact	

A WORLD OF A DIFFERENCE

THE TWELFTH PRINCIPLE

TEXT 3

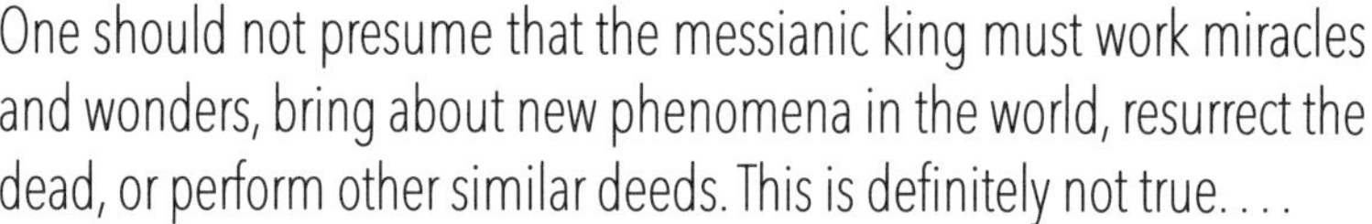

One should not presume that the messianic king must work miracles and wonders, bring about new phenomena in the world, resurrect the dead, or perform other similar deeds. This is definitely not true. . . .

If a king will arise from the House of David who diligently contemplates the Torah and observes its *mitzvot* as prescribed by the Written Law and the Oral Law as [King] David, his ancestor; will oblige all of Israel to walk in (the way of the Torah) and rectify the laxity in its observance; and fight the wars of God, we may, with assurance, consider him Mashiach. If he succeeds in the above, builds the Temple in its place, and gathers the dispersed of Israel, he is definitely the Mashiach.

He will then improve the entire world, motivating all the nations to serve God together, as Zephaniah 3:9 states: "I will transform the peoples to a purer language that they all will call upon the name of God and serve Him with one purpose."

Maimonides, *Mishneh Torah*, Laws of Kings 11:3-4

FIGURE 6.3

Myth	Mashiach must perform supernatural feats to be the redeemer.
Fact	

THE THIRTEENTH PRINCIPLE

TEXT 4

The resurrection of the dead is a foundation of the Torah of Moshe; one cannot maintain a connection to the Jewish religion without this belief.

Maimonides, *Commentary on Mishnah*, Introduction to *Perek Chelek*

KEY POINT

THE FINAL FRONTIER

UNITED AS ONE

KEY POINT

EXERCISE

What are the superficial purposes of the items in this list, and what are their true and holy purposes?

	Superficial Purpose	True Purpose
Food		
Sleep		
Socializing		
Vacation		
Work		

BACK TO THE FUTURE

TEXT 5

The reason God created the entire world, and the human being in particular, is because He "desired a home in the lower realms." That is, God wished that the "lower realms," namely, the physicality of this world, should become subservient to and a vehicle for expressing God. The purpose of Torah and *mitzvot* is to effect this transformation. . . . This is the reason why Torah and *mitzvot* are performed with physical objects by a soul vested in a physical body.

The Lubavitcher Rebbe, Rabbi Menachem M. Schneerson, *Igrot Kodesh* 2:67–68

KEY POINT

AWAKENING THE REDEMPTION

MASHIACH REVISITED

FIGURE 6.4

גולה	גאולה
Exile	Redemption

KEY POINT

TEXT 6

Redemption does not imply a departure from our current state—from our lives, routines, and world. To the contrary, the definition of redemption is that the very entity that was previously in a state of exile is—not nullified, God forbid, but—redeemed. . . . All the positive elements that are part of our current reality will remain intact; only their exilic condition will be eliminated. The concealment of each entity's true nature will be removed. . . .

This explains why the word *ge'ulah* (redemption) includes within itself the word *golah* (exile), with the added letter *alef*. Redemption will not do away with exile and our efforts therein. To the contrary, redemption's characteristic is that it lifts up and redeems the entire state of exile and transforms exile itself into redemption. This is done by removing all of exile's concealments, everything that obscures each thing's true nature and purpose, and revealing within everything the *alef,* which alludes to the Master *(aluf)* of the World. When we reveal the Master of the World in each thing—that is, the purpose for which God created it—then from exile itself, redemption emerges.

The Lubavitcher Rebbe, Rabbi Menachem M. Schneerson *Sefer Hasichot* 5751, 2:505–506

TEXT 7

שִׁיר הַמַּעֲלוֹת, בְּשׁוּב ה' אֶת שִׁיבַת צִיּוֹן הָיִינוּ כְּחֹלְמִים.

A song of ascents: When God returns the exiles to Zion, we [will realize that we] had been like dreamers.

Psalms 126:1

QUESTION FOR DISCUSSION

Why does King David not describe the redemption as a "dream come true," but rather that we will recall the earlier times of exile and we will realize that we had been dreaming?

FIGURE 6.5

Myth	The redemption is a prize God will grant us for hanging in there and sticking with Him for a few thousand years.
Fact	

THE PRINCIPLES APPLIED

KEY POINT

TEXT 8

A person should always view oneself as equally balanced with merits and faults, and view the world, too, as equally balanced with merits and faults. . . . Therefore, if one performs but one mitzvah, he tips the balance—his own and the entire world's—and effects personal and global deliverance and salvation.

Maimonides, *Mishneh Torah*, Laws of Repentance 3:4

FIGURE 6.6

The Seven Noahide Laws
1. Acknowledge that there is only one God.
2. Respect the Creator.
3. Do not murder.
4. Do not engage in illicit sexual behavior (e.g., incest and adultery).
5. Respect the property of others.
6. Do not cause unnecessary suffering to animals.
7. Maintain a judicial system to enforce these laws.

KEY POINT

ACKNOWLEDGMENTS

Myth Busters, an entertaining and thought-provoking course for Jewish teenagers, challenges common misconceptions about Judaism and provides participants with perspectives that will help them separate fact from fiction regarding their precious heritage. The course's primary objective is to dispel the myth that Judaism is disconnected from and not relevant to modern life.

Much of this course was adapted from JLI's *Fascinating Facts* course, authored by **Rabbi Avrohom Sternberg** and **Rivkah Slonim**. Lessons Four and Six of this course were also adapted from JLI's *Journey of the Soul*, authored by **Rabbi Naftali Silberberg**. **Rabbi Michoel Shapiro** modified these original materials to make them appropriate for a teenage audience. **Rabbis Mordechai Dinerman** and **Naftali Silberberg,** who ably head the JLI Curriculum Department, offered indispensable editorial support.

We thank **Rabbi Levke Kaplan**, director of operations at JLI Central, whose invaluable advice and devoted efforts guided the development of this course. We are grateful to **Rivki Mockin** for coordinating the many elements of course development and production.

We extend our appreciation to **Rabbi Zalman Abraham** who skillfully provides the vision for branding JLI course offerings. Heartfelt thanks to **Shevi Rivkin** for her assistance with producing the beautifully designed promotional and instructional materials.

We are grateful to **Mendel Schtroks** for designing the textbooks with taste, expertise, and patience, and **Rabbi Mendel Sirota** for directing book production. **Ya'akovah Weber and Reuvena Grodnitzky** enhanced the quality and professionalism of the course with their copyediting and proofreading. **Bunia Rapoport** designed the course's aesthetically pleasing PowerPoints.

Our deep gratitude is due to **Aliza Landes,** administrator of JLI Teens, for her dedication and commitment to our affiliates. Her efforts serve as the backbone of our program.

We acknowledge the hard work and efforts of JLI's support staff and administration, whose contributions to this course were critical, but whose names are too many to enumerate.

We are immensely grateful for the encouragement of JLI's visionary chairman and vice-chairman of Merkos L'Inyonei Chinuch–Lubavitch World Headquarters, **Rabbi Moshe Kotlarsky.** Rabbi Kotlarsky has been highly instrumental in building the infrastructure for the expansion of Chabad's international network and is the architect of scores of initiatives and services to help Chabad representatives across the globe succeed in their mission. We are blessed to have the unwavering support of JLI's principal benefactor, **Mr. George Rohr,** who is fully invested in our work and continues to be instrumental in JLI's monumental expansion.

Deep gratitude is due to the director of JLI, **Rabbi Efraim Mintz**, whose visionary leadership has set new standards of Jewish learning for adults, for teens, and for all of those that JLI serves. Thanks is also due to the JLI Teens' chairman, **Rabbi Chaim Block**, for his ongoing advice and counsel.

Inspired by the call of the **Lubavitcher Rebbe, Rabbi Menachem Mendel Schneerson,** of righteous memory, it is the mandate of the Rohr JLI to encourage all Jews throughout the world to experience and participate in their precious heritage of Torah learning. Through the JLI Teens Discovery Program, Jewish high school students of all levels of knowledge and background have a unique educational program that enables them to find personal meaning and relevance in the Torah's teachings. May their increased Torah learning, mitzvah observance, and dedication to shaping a brighter future for all humankind hasten the coming of the true and complete redemption.

Rabbi Elya Silfen
Director of JLI Teens
Brooklyn, New York
22 Shevat, 5776

NOTES

NOTES

The Jewish Learning Multiplex

Brought to you by the Rohr Jewish Learning Institute

In fulfillment of the mandate of the Lubavitcher Rebbe, of blessed memory, whose leadership guides every step of our work, the mission of the Rohr Jewish Learning Institute is to transform Jewish life and the greater community through the study of Torah, connecting each Jew to our shared heritage of Jewish learning.

While our flagship program remains the cornerstone of our organization, JLI is proud to feature additional divisions catering to specific populations, in order to meet a wide array of educational needs.

THE ROHR JEWISH LEARNING INSTITUTE,
a subsidiary of *Merkos L'Inyonei Chinuch*,
is the adult education arm of the Chabad-Lubavitch Movement.

Torah Studies provides a rich and nuanced encounter with the weekly Torah reading.

MyShiur courses are designed to assist students in developing the skills needed to study Talmud independently.

This rigorous fellowship program invites select college students to explore the fundamentals of Judaism.

Jewish teens forge their identity as they engage in Torah study, social interaction, and serious fun.

The Rosh Chodesh Society gathers Jewish women together once a month for intensive textual study.

TorahCafe.com provides an exclusive selection of top-rated Jewish educational videos.

This yearly event rejuvenates mind, body, and spirit with a powerful synthesis of Jewish learning and community.

Participants delve into our nation's rich past while exploring the Holy Land's relevance and meaning today.

Select affiliates are invited to partner with peers and noted professionals, as leaders of innovation and excellence.

Machon Shmuel is an institute providing Torah research in the service of educators worldwide.